The Secret Ministry

Tim Dooley

Smith/Doorstop Books

Published 2001 by
Smith/Doorstop Books
The Poetry Business
The Studio
Byram Arcade
Westgate
Huddersfield HD1 1ND

Copyright © Tim Dooley
All Rights Reserved

ISBN 1-902382-34-X
Typeset at The Poetry Business
Printed by Swiftprint, Huddersfield

The Poetry Business gratefully acknowledges the help of
Kirklees Metropolitan Council and Yorkshire Arts.

Acknowledgements
Some of these poems have appeared previously in the following publications: *Ambit, Dog, Numbers, The North, Poetry London Newsletter, The Rialto, Sheffield Thursday, Southern Review* (USA), *Swansea Review, Tears in the Fence, Times Literary Supplement, Verse.*
'Brief Encounter' won fourth prize in the City of Cardiff International Poetry Competition, 1992. A short selection was runner-up for the Blue Nose Poet of the Year Competition, 1997.

CONTENTS

5	Sleepwalker's Romance
6	June
7	Preparing to meet the day
8	The Sound We Make Ourselves
9	Afterwards
10	The Border
11	Aspinall's Zoo
12	Heritage
13	Breakdown
13	Disturbance
14	Another Part of the City
15	Edit
16	Nightfall
19	Brief Encounter
20	Directive
21	Out
22	Détente
23	Tityus
24	The Secret Ministry
26	Revenants
28	The Milky Way
30	Working from Home

for Sam and Ben

SLEEPWALKER'S ROMANCE

Shoes were at the heart of it. That much was clear.
Luxurious shoes of all-assuaging suppleness.
And he had left them there. Wherever there was.
With the picnic stuff in the precinct or the shopping bags
on the hilltop. And now he was here. And here
was also subject to change at a moment's notice.
The back of a Morris Minor or the restaurant at Fortnum's.
But wherever here was, they were. Welcome and comforting.
His children. His parents. This or that beloved?
But the only shoes on offer were a pair of beat-up trainers.
Not Reeboks exactly. Never mind the fur-lined slipper.
So he had to head off along the hostile corridors.
The playground was wet and it was becoming dark
earlier than expected. And there were questions to answer.
He realised that by now someone else could have the shoes.
And he might never know if it was power or it was love.
That he was running from. That he was searching out.

JUNE

The first weeks of Wimbledon
and the word 'love'
has passed between us like
zero, or some chosen
absolute. That ochre picture
– sunpainted Italy –
a trail snapped from a mountain
in your teens, now
stained by late development
is in my eye again.

Those first times away from him
look empty and unfinished,
as we sort your father's things
and the word 'alone'
opens like a blister in the earth.

PREPARING TO MEET THE DAY

A routine and a rite –
this soaping, scraping away
of the night's crop of maleness.

Rinsing the blade,
as if concealing the evidence –

he catches, in the air,
rank nicotine and silence.

His hand on her shoulder
is no help at all.

A relic from that time
they looked together at the light
we move through, and towards.

THE SOUND WE MAKE OURSELVES

                A tamed assault-
course. This latest in play furniture; climbing frames
                    of slatted pine,
tyre steps, a ladder bridge and – almost
                    at arm's length
and harmless below the enflamed trees –
                    the sun's quiet fire
returning some coolness in our stare.

                A week ago,
on Broadwater Farm – as, once, in Divis Flats
                    front doors collapsed
at dawn to our concern. Like uniformed men,
                    stepping over
a woman who may or may not be dying,
                    we are vague
about detail and take slowly to speech.

                We're catching up
on other news, old friendship calling back
                    a flickering warmth.
In the hall of the home you're outgrowing:
                    a daughter's picture,
the rings of paint she added to your work
                    and jagged drawings
done with the left hand, against habits of style.

                Yesterday,
light like this caught a three-foot profile
                    on the green canal
as my son stopped to listen on our walk and said,
                    he heard two things:
the bird's expected music in the trees and,
                    what I'd not heard,
our shoe steps crashing through the new crisp leaves.

AFTERWARDS

The ritual of open-evening wall-displays.
In the maths corridor, she came on neatly-shaded graphs,
histograms, colour-coded pies. *Our Leisure Time.*
TV, homework, shopping, sports and games
jostling with visits to friends and paper rounds.

On Raymond's bar chart, a single column towered above
its neighbours' dwarfish blocks, its simple label *Out.*
It didn't take her long to bring to life from that
an image of the gangly, crop-haired boy, dangling
on a swing too small for him, in the wet and leafstrewn park.

And it seems no time has passed when, in an unfamiliar pub,
a voice calls out, *Remember me, Miss!*
He tells her how he went back to show them all:
his uniform, the noise his boots made on the tiling floors.
Mr. Jones said, let us know before, another time.

He expected Ireland, got the Gulf. *There's lots of stuff
you never hear about. This big ditch we dug ...* Afterwards
he got out quick. Health reasons. But the training gets you work.
Security. Firearms' research. *But I was always clumsy, Miss.*
He gestures with his splintered lower arm.

THE BORDER

The queue might take an hour we're told.
Meanwhile, there's this form to fill, a relic of the recent past.
Currency, traveller's cheques, purpose of visit.
On the seat behind, you doze at last,
your glasses slipping down your nose,
the adventure discarded on your lap,
crumpled between your elbow and the seat.

It's your birthday and we're crossing to a new landscape.
This morning we saw harvests piled on rolling plains,
the chimneys of collective bakeries,
sheds where cattle live out secret lives indoors.
Now the afternoon unfolds on strips of field
where horses pull a plough
and hay's stooked in tidy decorated sheaves.

They put up the signs to Helsinki
the year that you were born. We watched
hesitant steps break into a confident
uneven run, the beginnings of self-control.
New choices will be made, unmaking the past,
and you, half-grown, rub your eyes awake
to a new country, another year in which to live.

ASPINALL'S ZOO

A four year-old's arm
raised to point out
the big cat slavering
on the long sloping bough.

That half term holiday,
our first year of teaching,
crazy with the shock of failure
we'd escaped to Kent.

How vulnerable the fences
seemed. The monkeys,
grieving disturbed adolescents,
threw shit at the laughing crowd.

It was that Sunday the hours change:
the evenings suddenly darker,
the animals' food unexpectedly late.

It took a decade to cope with the job,
another to study each other.

And every few years
these stories in the papers:
dismembered limbs,
loyal keepers' widows,
the stale excuses
of Lucky Lucan's friend.

HERITAGE

On the beach, elements
stutter in Greek – we're
pebble philosophers –

My father would pitch
a flat one spinning
to skip once, twice …
across uplifting water.

My sons and I
just feed the waves
like keepers tossing meat.

BREAKDOWN

It must be the longest time I've spent
in Lancashire. Fingernails touch-type
formica as we see through flecked glass
a prune and cream bus on a bridge.

The roofless mills: Nelson like Rievaulx.
A man about my age says that green swathe
by the canal bank was factories once.
Bare ruination. The train refuses to begin.

DISTURBANCE

Responsible authority
looks into thefts of
bandages and bottles.

At the word *agitation*
my hands begin to tremble
like someone made to speak.

ANOTHER PART OF THE CITY

It was dark. He was wet and half a mile west
of where he was meant to be. So he dried out,
nursing a pint of mottled, off-brown best
in the back lounge of a bar that had been named
for some Crimean battle. The street had been lined
with recent cars and fairly healthy trees.

Inside was the usual plush, brasses and polished
wood – and the usual talk he supposed: office
politics, purchases, a hint about creosote, the match;
and an odd running joke about a man called Pritchard.
Pritchard was nothing to him. He would never get the hang
of his story, never know why Godalming was funny or important.

He had tried Pork Scratchings, tried an interest in cricket.
Now he sat with his back to the wall and a pencil
for the crossword. It was beginning to trickle through –
what Eva had told him at the party in Dulwich.
What it means for your face not to fit. To be moon-featured
or differently complexioned, with the magazines gorgeously gaunt.

Or what Gregor had said about his first trip back
in the early days of the thaw. Exhausting welcomes
and a bloke who could tell from his face the exact suburb
his father and uncle had fled from. Not particularly clever.
You needn't know anything about visas or fear – just where the Jews
were likely to have lived. He was getting the message.

It was dark. He was dry, but half a mile west
of where he was meant to be. So he drained down
the remains of his mottled, off-brown best
and left his paper, clueless, on the sagging chair.
It was just that he was off course. Not the weather,
not the map. Pritchard, Godalming. And unfamiliar trees.

EDIT

You could start rumours about rivals and substantiate them.
Invert the corporate planner's wall-chart. Secrete his fresh
pack of Post-Its in the marketing manager's drawer.
Then wait for the many-headed snake to do its surreptitious worst,
insinuating between desk and VDU, sliding behind vertical files,
past the *monstera* no-one bothered to water.
Prepare to profit, to be amused, to forget the whole thing.

At the end of lunch, instead of getting up from the table, and sneaking
half-reluctantly like the others back to your parking place,
linger with that magnificent she or he who switched the earth's magnetic
poles back then. Stay all afternoon, with a print
of the harbour at Mykonos, some fruit and drying bread.
Stay after the serious drinking, the singing, the talk of running away.
Stay as the foolish drinking starts.

But it would be wrong!
Some repeated phrase or loop you didn't recognise straight off.
As you sand your palms with stubble, facing the washroom mirror,
it becomes monstrously clear that this is Nixon's voice.
The background's different silence
tells you the phrase was recorded later,
spliced into the tape to disguise guilt.

NIGHTFALL

Throughout autumn, all through the graduated,
creeping grey of journeys past the railway bridge,
Lucille noted days on which
light kept its promises – great
blocks of pale or darker blue
offset by russets, lemons or maroons.
Businesses thrived or closed. Beggars sang tunes
or sold cheap lighters. She watched the sky for change
until it seemed she reached the end of change.

Darkening days lit up with festivals,
fireworks for Diwali or Guy Fawkes.
Week-ends meant shorter, damper walks,
or trips to newly opened malls
outside the city limits.
This week new Beaujolais. All the next,
displays of party dresses. Under lights,
in air-warmed atria, she felt as if on stage,
as if what haunted her was just a stage

to pass through like the others. Winter colds
hung on longer than before. Foggy air
left stains on the windscreen of her car.
All of it made her feel old
suddenly. Outside, an
ear-ringed, peak-capped boy played *Nowhere Man,*
his dog wrapped in a neat plaid blanket. And
Happy Christmas (War is Over) played again
in the lift to the parking floors. And again

small nations' griefs plumped up the weekend press.
Each widow's grief was different and the same.
Each mother's horror measured as
a fractured smile, a face undressed.

Lucille put on her mask,
set out to face the early evening's tasks,
thought again how much the year had asked
of her. At the street's end stood the sky:
the overbearing, weighty, hardened sky.

The dashboard LCD read **16:12**.
Tall orange streetlights started to come on.
Behind them, sulphurous yellow ran
its course beneath the groaning shelf
of cloud that thickened still.
Is this how dark it gets? The question Lucille
asked could penetrate the crystalline array
of solid surfaces, enter a space
an angstrom wide, or reach to distant space,

interrogating emptiness of galaxies,
asking non-decreasing event horizons
what light comes in or out. Reasons,
arguments – the stuff exegeses
explore – implode near
a black hole's neither light nor darkened door;
and interstellar spaces no longer hoard
a crown of candles, or some freakish star.
Lucille looked at the clouded night which no star

burst through. Inside houses, coloured balls
cheered wrecked conifers, families found meaning
in games or company. Nothing
egregious disturbed decked halls.
Lucille dropped out of sight.
Without her, little changed. The sky grew lighter
a little longer as the year turned. White
petals broke the soil's crust – the grave of all
kept its secrets … almost like nothing at all.

BRIEF ENCOUNTER

Bonking in Rome,
Goethe tapped hexameters on his mistress's back.
O'Driscoll thought of home,
listening out for the tickety-clack
of rail and wheel that wasn't to be heard
in the air-conditioned carriage.

His fingers worked a brief massage
through the shaggy beard that just
resisted grey. Then a quick
double slap to the cheeks, to wake
himself – or get the touch at least
of something real.

He turned his gaze away from the rail
to the imaginary face
of Eva, his companion. She traced
a letter in the moistened vapour
you don't get in trains these days. *J'ai peur,*
she would have said, had she been French.

But she was American. And language
loped away from her in long arching swirls,
even and intelligent,
naming what went past, examining what was meant
by the latest curl and turn
in what was surely not the march of events.

O'Driscoll considered a sandwich,
observed a chalk horse stretched out against
ancient greenery, and thought
of generations who crept down from hill-forts
to scrape the grass away – their unfenced
world – and what he still called the mind of Man.

The flare of Eva's lucent mind
guttered momently; and he was rising, breathless,
to the story of that Dorset giant, taller
than some cathedrals, with its enormous ... *No, a phallus,*
she intercepted briefly,
a penis is a great deal smaller.

And he had made her up to cut him down.
Fantastic irony. The train stayed on the track.
All he could do was read his paperback,
sharing romantic sorrows with Young Werther.

DIRECTIVE

There will be no dogs.
Muscle relaxant techniques developed in the clean cities campaign
to go national. Private sponsorship will match
innovation capital in sheep-herding areas.

The public role of Corgis to be phased out.
Also increased competition for heritage manufacturers.
Alternatives to Elgar to be encouraged.
The new anthem: *A Nation now and then.*

The new religion: spiritualism.
Replace that back-street, ouija-tapping fraud
with a customer-focused chain. Agree quality thresholds
for contact with the dead, service length and ectoplasm.

And horticulture rationalised.
The unlovely rose uprooted, its antisocial thorns burnt on hilltop beacons,
seeds pulverised, different-shaded petals shredded,
making the land free for order and light.

OUT

Lucille had the letter in her bag and *gratitude, rightsize,
leaner strategy,* corkscrewed in her mind,
as she took the stairs in twos, took the leave owing her,
left quickly, taking the stairs again, in no particular order.
She took the tube to where she'd left the car,
slunk in and, glancing up and left,
moved into traffic. She ventured vaguely northward.
Kilburn State, the Welsh Harp reservoir, slipped past to one side.
When Jazz FM faded, she scrambled, one hand in the shoe box,
for a tape. Not Gorecki. Not Neil Young Unplugged.
She fished for the cassette Khaleb had taped in Cairo.
Umm Khaltoun's plaintive singing. Rhythm and voice
passionate, unyielding, unintelligible to her
as she blocked out Hertfordshire. She found herself
in Hitchin, paid and displayed, considered her position, found
nothing useful to her but a poached egg and tea.
And yet continued, eastwards now, garden-ribbon pseudo-cities
opening to tall skies of the broad East Anglian plain
somewhere near Wallington, where Eric Blair was wed
and saw, near Manor Farm, a cart horse bullied by a boy.
She skirted Cambridge heading North, suppressing a regret,
attaining speed on dual-carriage A-roads,
dodging horse-boxes, seeing airfields to her right, slowing
to fields in harvest and Swaffham's Georgian square,
still unsatisfied, still not knowing what she sought.
Near Walsingham an older world erupted:
Gothic arches bare as neolithic bones, prayer-filled,
sanctimonious sanctuaries. She shivered, heading for the coast.
Between Wells-next-Sea and Sheringham, she bought
a ticket for the motor boat that takes you out
into the brown waters south of Blakeney Point,
where oyster catchers dive for food
and the diamond-glittering, brown-and-grey-skinned seals,
swivel and swim between sand bank and Arctic sound,
nurturing their young, adapting like the coastline to the tide.

DÉTENTE

A fingertip at play
inside you and my head
cushioned on your breast,
listening like a safebreaker
for some loosening
of the latch.

The thin ice has melted
on the lake and they've unlocked
the bridge to the small island
where rock plants flower – saxifrage,
or snowdrops waving tiny
flags of truce.

TITYUS

In Michelangelo's drawing
this voluptuous male reclines,
one hand tied to a pillow of stone
while the other seems to slide below
the belly of the broad-spanned,
muscular, soft-feathered bird.
Daily it pecks his liver,
sensuality's last square.
Nightly his strength returns.

Stanley walks around the frame
to see the figure traced again.
On the verso it emerges
a resurrected Christ.

On a preserved railway platform,
a dozen years ago,
he saw a kiss between women:
a face upturned, something
half suppressed, half understood,
hanging like steam in air,
compressed like veins in rock.

THE SECRET MINISTRY

Šumplica Novakova laughed
as she zigzagged from queue to queue
in the cabbage market,
her last purchase always
the braided poppy-seed rolls.
Her bright silk blouses –
lilac, crimson or whichever colour
her hidden calendar required –
lightened the day,
when she broke and shared the eucharist
among carefully invited friends.

When a mate from the plant
made a fool of himself with a girl,
I'd invite him home for a meal.
He'd meet Jinka and the kids.
We'd drink a few beers, eat dumplings
and meat seasoned with a herb
that might recall his wife's name.
I gave absolution under my breath,
making a sign in the palm of my hand.

Now they've given the postal workers
museum back to the Cistercians.
I've a collar to wear and memos
from Rome about Mexican practices.
The lads are friendly enough,
but look at me
like a guy with something to sell,
some multinational's rep.

Last week, I saw Šumplica
in the marketplace,
finding the best fruit
as ever. Once, she whispered
what would not be silenced.
Now, she spoke out loud,
steadying her bicycle. It was
after all, love we ministered to
so no regrets. She laughed
as the pigeons scattered,
flying off God knows where.

REVENANTS

i.m. E. Farrants

It's this same train-rattled flat
that we find shelter in, after
a Bohemian summer storm, presaged by
dust-devils, cloud cover
and sudden corridors of wind.

The fretted rail of vine leaves
that framed our balcony has gone.
The cane chairs we left behind, seatless,
sprout long tendrils; they've lost
whatever strawberry or pistachio tint

made our neighbours covet them.
Against cracked plaster and bared stone,
a pear-tree has wound round the towering beech
in next door's abandoned garden.
Six meters up, it offers hard and tasteless fruit.

The broken-backed damp books
are Pavel's, who kept the place
through the barely breaking winter of our
London years. I take down
Hrabal's *I Served the King of England* and recall

a Saturday in Kew, the
year that he could visit us;
how Pavel pulled his loping form up the
wrought-iron spiral stair
to view the largest indoor plant in Europe,

touching the roof of the temperate house.
His vaulted cheekbones, his eyes
clear, blue, transparent as the sky through glass,
shaded by the foppish brim
of his unseasonal panama. Return won't bring

the great release we dreamed of
any more than exile did.
Faces altered by disease, age, or merely compromise
greet us back in Prague.
But summer storms end quickly here.

And, as in London, we seek
refuge in iron fantasies
of the Belle Époque: Petřin Hill's pastiche
of the Eiffel tower,
or the hall of mirrors where versions of our selves,

mis-shaped, repeat themselves
in mocking parallels.
The bright blue eyes of the soldier across from us
on yesterday's train
shone under the blue of his United Nations cap,

as Pavel's did at Kew.
Fates that ensnare enchant us first.
The sketchbook on your knee awaits defining lines.
Light and shade to draw the moment
from its labyrinth, to still a resisting heart.

THE MILKY WAY

The marble features of the Parthenon frieze
        aren't the only things
to seem flatter and greyer since the summer
        you were sixteen.

O'Driscoll remembers the white bicycles
        those other Provos
left on Amsterdam street corners for free
        and common use.

There were pictures from museums on the train
        and songs of that time
in the background, the five days we crossed
        from the Stedelijk

to Jordaan's brown cafés. It was later though,
        with wanted posters
for the Red Army Fraction pasted on a wall
        at the terminus.

There were screams in the night, soft cheese
        and jam at breakfast.
A tape of Bukka White barely troubled the
        glittering meniscus

of your genever, or the couple chopping a black
        cube into silver-
paper deals: their downy daughter snoozing
        on the bar.

We shared a four bunk room with transients
        waiting to buy a car.

Stavros and his cousin were ready to go home
           – after a decade

in New York, struggling with electronics and
           English, repairing
beat-up radios, lecturing on Ritsos – to go home
           to the free use

of their tongue. O'Driscoll is easing his way
           into the story
of his second time in Holland – peace week
           at the Melkweg.

Did his disarmament play leave the audience stunned
           or were they stoned,
like the actors, staring at significant intervals
           between words?

He wants to tell us about the boat-trip back to Hull,
           how they disposed
of the stuff – fear and the North Sea at night.
           I am looking

in your eyes at a different year and the dark
           sea off Naxos,
a high glittering sky and its reflection,
           like a window

opening in our marriage, the evening's gifts
           scattered freely,
like the broad and unmourned highway
           of spilt milk.

WORKING FROM HOME

    Watching, through the open
French doors and conservatory glass, these birds queuing
    at the feeder, pecking
and spitting out nuts and seeds, submissively anointing
    their forefeathers
in the drinking bowl, I tidy a table, content with
    what's brought us here:
times of waiting or worry, or losing our patience,
    and days like these
when someone takes the children out and someone stays
    with papers to read.
One day you're at the wave-pool. Spread out on the floor
    are coursework folders:
teenage fiction, research on street-gangs, someone's response
    to Wesker's *Roots*
and Hamid's painful, broken story of escaping from Tehran.
    Shootings, disappearances,
a Pepsi Cola lorry overturned, unclean, its sticky bubbly fluid
    running in the streets.
Another day you're working. In the Science Museum
    Sam, Benedict and I
start the combine harvester, make counterweights for bridges
    or launch a rocket.
Inside one case an Edsel; further on the crooked foot-digger
    Hebridean crofters
called a caschcrom. By raising or lowering a handle,
    those too poor to plough
determined the depth of the groove they needed to cut
    in the sparse soil,
then gripped the wooden shaft and kick-started the share.
    I was writing some review

that Saturday you and the children went to London Zoo.
            Waiting in line
for llama rides, you thought you recognised the smiling, neat
            and prematurely balding man
holding his son's hand just ahead, steadying him in the cart.
            It turned out not to be,
you realised on the train coming home, another parent
            from the local school,
but the man who'd won the Booker Prize for *Midnight's Children*.
            That was years ago, of course,
and now you're upstairs writing a reference for a nurse
            in your Literature class,
while I chop onions and listen for our not quite warring sons.
            Though the author of *Shame*
might fear to be seen with a child in public now, though the enclosing,
            impoverishing mind
shouts 'Kill the Ba'hais' or plans forced migrations, at evening
            perennial birdsong
brightens our garden. It doesn't make everything right, but
            makes it easier,
the children bathed and read to, easier to touch another's hand,
            or speak quietly,
so when night does come what we notice is an arc of moonlight
            curved by the ribbed
plastic roof above us – no rainbow or triumphal arch, but
            what work tends toward –
efforts of love: attention, desire, holding darkness at bay.

Tim Dooley has taught in and near London since 1974. He is head of English at Rickmansworth School, Hertfordshire. He has reviewed contemporary poetry extensively, particularly for the *TLS*, and has a research MA on the poetry of Clough from the Open University. He lives in Harrow with his wife and two sons.

He won the Sheffield Thursday Poetry Prize in 1995.

His full length collection, *The Interrupted Dream*, was published by Anvil in 1985.

This collection was a winner in The Poetry Business Book & Pamphlet Competition 2000